THE ADMINISTRATIVE ASSISTANT

Brenda Bailey-Hughes

A FIFTY-MINUTE™ SERIES BOOK

CRISP PUBLICATIONS, INC.
Menlo Park, California

THE ADMINISTRATIVE ASSISTANT

by
Brenda Bailey-Hughes

CREDITS
Managing Editor: **Kathleen Barcos**
Editor: **Amy Marks**
Production: **Barbara Atmore**
Typesetting: **ExecuStaff**
Cover Design: **Carol Harris**

Copyright © 1998 by Crisp Publications, Inc.
Printed in the United States of America by Bawden Printing Company.

www.crisplearning.com

Distribution to the U.S. Trade:

National Book Network, Inc.
4720 Boston Way
Lanham, MD 20706
1-800-462-6420

99 00 01 02   10 9 8 7 6 5 4 3 2

Library of Congress Catalog Card Number 97-69693
Brenda Bailey-Hughes
The Administrative Assistant
ISBN 1-56052-456-1

This book is printed on recyclable paper with soy ink.

LEARNING OBJECTIVES FOR:

THE ADMINISTRATIVE ASSISTANT

The objectives for *The Administrative Assistant* are listed below. They have been developed to guide you, the reader, to the core issues covered in this book.

Objectives

- ❏ **1) To discuss the responsibilities of the administrative assistant**

- ❏ **2) To resolve communication problems**

- ❏ **3) To deal with supervisory situations**

- ❏ **4) To discuss problems and special concerns**

Assessing Your Progress

In addition to the learning objectives, Crisp, Inc. has developed an **assessment** that covers the fundamental information presented in this book. A twenty-five item, multiple choice/true-false question-naire allows the reader to evaluate his or her comprehension of the subject matter. An answer sheet with a chart matching the questions to the listed objectives is also available. To learn how to obtain a copy of this assessment, please call **1-800-442-7477** and ask to speak with a Customer Service Representative.

Assessments should not be used in any selection process.

ABOUT THE AUTHOR

Brenda Baily-Hughes conducts a variety of training workshops for support staff of universities and business organizations. She coordinates a twelve-month series for the support staff of Indiana University covering a variety of personal and professional development topics. Brenda has written a variety of published short stories. *The Administrative Assistant* is her first book.

CONTENTS

CONTENTS (continued)

Introduction

WHO IS THE ADMINISTRATIVE ASSISTANT?

Have you ever tried to describe the career of an administrative assistant to someone? How would you respond to someone asking, "An administrative assistant? What's that?" Many of the familiar terms, such as secretary or office manager, are simply not an accurate description of all that the professional assistant does. In fact, if the assistant were to explain all that is done on a daily or weekly basis, it would probably take a day or a week to describe! The administrative assistant supports the activities of one or more managers or executives. Consequently, nearly anything that falls within the parameters of the boss's job also ends up on the assistant's plate. The administrative assistant has a broad spectrum of responsibilities, and the spectrum just keeps growing.

As middle management downsizes, administrative assistants find themselves taking on more and more responsibility. Increased responsibilities create pressure and work overload, but don't be fooled—administrative assistants across the nation love their emerging role in the business world! How do you envision the ideal administrative role for yourself?

Imagine that you have landed the perfect position as an administrative assistant. You're at a social gathering of some sort. People are mingling about in a comfortable environment, and you and I bump into each other. We introduce ourselves and begin chatting. You mention what a crazy day it was at the office today. "Oh really," I say. "What do you do?"

Think carefully for a moment, and write down your response. Describe an administrative assistant role as you would like it to be.

_____

_____

_____

_____

Contemplating the ideal administrative assistant position may be far more important than you realize. As you describe your ideal role you begin creating a vision of what you can be. Articulating a bold, creative vision is the first step in achieving it.

CHECKLIST OF RESPONSIBILITIES

Let's begin with a look at some of the most common responsibilities of an administrative assistant. Place a check next to any tasks for which you currently have responsibility. Write in your additional tasks not found on the list.

Assist Managers

❑ attend meetings

❑ complete routine correspondence for managers

❑ plan speeches

❑ respond to much of managers' correspondence

❑ schedule appointments for managers

❑ serve on committees

❑ make travel arrangements

Supervise Office Operations and Support Staff

❑ hire

❑ assign work

❑ create absence reports

❑ arrange for transfers

❑ make dismissals

❑ plan and coordinate meetings and conferences

❑ train

❑ make merit and pay recommendations

❑ manage payroll

❑ coordinate vacation schedules

❑ serve as computer coordinator

    ❑ evaluate software and hardware

    ❑ draft proposals

    ❑ manage installations

- ❏ monitor incoming mail

- ❏ identify needs and develop administrative policy and procedures

- ❏ coordinate special projects (e.g., establish databases, create job procedure manuals)

- ❏ plan and schedule departmental functions such as award ceremonies and luncheons

- ❏ maintain and organize files

- ❏ coordinate building maintenance

- ❏ coordinate equipment maintenance

- ❏ edit copy for printed materials

- ❏ review and approve accuracy and completeness of all departmental forms

- ❏ coordinate preparation and production of promotional materials

- ❏ serve as account manager

  - ❏ approve purchases

  - ❏ verify expenditures

  - ❏ reconcile expenditures

  - ❏ provide instruction on budget procedures

  - ❏ initiate budget transfers

  - ❏ assimilate data for budget preparation

  - ❏ prepare various budget reports

  - ❏ project needs and prepare budgetary requests

- ❏ assist in long-range planning for the department

CHECKLIST OF RESPONSIBILITIES
(continued)

Provide Information

- ❏ serve as resource person and act to resolve administrative problems

- ❏ answer inquiries by phone, in person and in writing

- ❏ serve as liaison to public and other departments

- ❏ collect information and compile data for publications and reports

- ❏ edit and write various departmental publications

- ❏ prepare a variety of statistical reports and analyses reflecting department activities

- ❏ prepare contracts and supporting documentation

    - ❏ conduct research

    - ❏ make calculations

    - ❏ prepare rough drafts

Other responsibilities unique to your position:

- ❏ _____

- ❏ _____

- ❏ _____

- ❏ _____

We will return to this checklist for additional insights. Right now look (and be amazed) at all you can do! The administrative assistant role is growing every day and offers exciting career opportunities for those with a vision for the position.

In the following chapters we will explore the five key skill areas for success as an administrative assistant:

1. Managing multiple roles (wearing many hats)

2. Assisting the manager

3. Supervising office operations and support staff

4. Providing information

5. Managing special concerns

C H A P T E R

1

Wearing Many Hats

MANAGING MULTIPLE ROLES

Looking over the Checklist of Responsibilities (pages 4–6), you can see that the administrative assistant wears many hats. Becoming proficient at each of the various roles is a difficult task. As challenging, is being able to switch hats from one role to another as necessary. As you read the different scenario on page 12 think about these questions: What hats is Pat wearing? What hats should she have been wearing? How could Pat shift more successfully from one role to another?

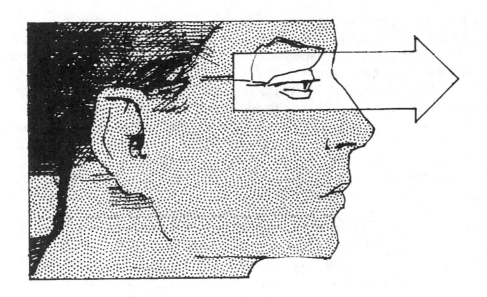

Switching Hats

Pat is a hard-working assistant in a corporate organization. She supervises the receptionist and assists the department director and three managers. Her technical skills (typing, filing, computer skills, and so on) are above average, yet she receives only average performance evaluations.

Pat begins her day at 8:00 A.M. sharp. She launches immediately into typing a document that had been left on her desk the night before. At about 8:30 A.M. the director and managers start arriving. Pat continues typing. The director, Ms. McInnery comes out of her office and stands near Pat's desk, watching her. After about 30 seconds, Pat turns to the director and raises one eyebrow. Ms. McInnery says, "Sorry to interrupt. I know you are very busy. Do you know where the list of books under review is?" Pat replies, "Sorry, haven't seen it," and returns to her typing. Ms. McInnery returns to her office.

Pat finishes typing the document at around 9:00 A.M. and puts it in Mr. Sanchez's mailbox. The office is officially open to customers now, and Sheila, the receptionist, is supposed to be there to take calls and greet walk-ins. She is not. Customer traffic and phone calls begin to pick up. Pat forwards to the managers the calls from customers wanting to know office hours, forwards to the director the calls from vendors selling new products and forwards to Customer Relations the requests for information from prospective customers. She is courteous and efficient with each caller. She handles walk-in traffic with equal deftness, although the physical presence of a customer seems to lengthen the time necessary to complete a transaction.

With only one customer in the waiting area and the phones momentarily quiet, Pat returns to her in-basket. Ms. Huckleberry has asked Pat to draft a memo. Pat ponders over what to write, how to say it and what format to use. She finally puts the request back in her in-box, mutters that she wished Ms. Huckleberry would do her own "darned writing" and moves on to photocopying requests.

Sheila arrives at 9:45 A.M. She launches into a long, detailed account of the previous evening, which included a flat tire, an injured cat, and a less-than-sober boyfriend. Pat listens carefully and responds by saying that it sounded like "a rough night."

Mr. Sanchez stops by to empty his mailbox. "Thanks for this book review list. I didn't realize you would have it done so quickly," he comments. "Have a nice day." Pat and Sheila respond in kind.

Identify the hats Pat wore. What hats, roles, or assistance would have been more productive? Compare your responses to those suggested on page 14.

_____

_____

_____

_____

_____

_____

SUGGESTED RESPONSES

Pat is missing numerous opportunities to provide valuable assistance to her department. She is limiting her position by functioning much as an entry-level secretary would operate.

1. Pat arrives and launches into a specific task without taking time to plan the day, anticipate needs or touch base with her manager. She needed to wear her office manager/planner hat.

2. When Ms. McInnery asked for a lost item Pat should have switched from typing to a detective hat or problem-solving role.

3. Pat's interaction with Ms. McInnery illustrates a lack of balance between people orientation and task orientation. The outstanding administrative assistant accomplishes necessary tasks without sacrificing pleasantness and helpfulness.

4. Pat is wearing a receptionist/switchboard operator hat as she transfers all calls. How many of those calls might she have answered, problems might she have resolved, customers might she have satisfied had she taken time to listen to callers before transferring them?

5. Pat doesn't recognize her customer service obligation. Customers are treated as transactions rather than the lifeblood of the organization.

6. Pat appears willing to do data entry or basic typing but is frustrated by Ms. Huckleberry's request that she compose a memo. Pat needed to switch gears to a more creative hat. (Switching from a logical, linear task to a creative task is easier if you take a break, walk about, talk with people or doodle.)

7. Pat needed to put on the supervisor hat when Sheila arrived. Good listening skills are important but so is constructive feedback about performance. Sheila needs to know that arriving exceptionally late is not acceptable.

8. Did you notice the document that Pat was typing for Mr. Sanchez? Could that be the same document that Ms. McInnery was looking for earlier? Pat missed being a valuable assistant because she wasn't looking at the big picture.

WHAT HATS DO OTHERS SEE YOU WEARING?

Administrative assistants across the nation are taking on increasing levels of responsibility, wearing more complex hats and contributing to the success of their organizations. Unfortunately, that contribution is not always recognized. The administrative assistant position is a new or expanded function in many companies. People may not understand the scope and level of an assistant's responsibilities. Carefully consider the language used to describe an assistant's function. Menial language may limit how others perceive the administrative assistant's abilities.

The following phrases have been rewritten to communicate the complexity of the task or the level of skill required to complete it.

FROM MENIAL: ⇨	TO MEANINGFUL:
Type a memo ⇨	Compose memos
Set up a meeting ⇨	Coordinate events
Sort mail ⇨	Prioritize communications
Call an angry customer ⇨	Manage customer relations
Help someone who can't print from the computer ⇨	Troubleshoot computer issues
Order supplies ⇨	Make purchasing decisions

This may appear to be mere wordsmithing or a semantic game, but communicating your level of responsibility is critical to your success. Administrators who hear an assistant refer to decision making, troubleshooting, or prioritizing are more likely to entrust that assistant with increased levels of responsibility. Don't allow ignorance or misunderstandings of your abilities limit your contribution to the organization.

WHAT YOUR MANAGER EXPECTS

When working as an assistant to a director or manager you will need to work hard to clarify expectations, to satisfy work-style preferences and to see the big picture.

Clarify Expectations

Clarify expectations when you first begin working with a manager (or managers). Explain the full range of activities to which you can provide support. Administrative assistants in different companies assume very different levels of responsibility. Do not assume that a new manager knows what you can do. Remember to use language that describes the full scope of your abilities. Ask the manager how your skills can be best utilized. If you've been with the same manager for a while, this may be a good time to reexamine the role you play. Consider the following questions:

Would a shift in your activities benefit the manager and the department? Why?

_____

_____

_____

What does your manager expect of you?

_____

_____

_____

What do you expect of an administrative assistant position?

_____

_____

_____

The clearer you and your boss are about responsibilities and expectations, the better your chance of success.

Work-Style Preferences

All individuals have work-style preferences that an assistant can support. The boss may have a distinct preference for mail that is opened or unopened; doors open or shut; phone calls announced or forwarded directly; voice mail, e-mail, or written messages; first names or titles. A manager may be a morning or an afternoon person. As the assistant becomes more sensitive and responsive to these preferences the support will be more individualized and more appreciated.

Think for a moment about the people you support. List individual preferences that you can begin to support:

Example:

Name of Manager	Preferences	Support Action
Jane Doe	Likes Geneva font and page numbers centered at bottom of page	Tell her I will use that format unless she notes otherwise.
	Likes having plenty of information while traveling	Attach phone numbers, directions and files to her travel agenda.

Name of Manager	Preferences	Support Action

WHAT YOUR MANAGER EXPECTS
(continued)

Name of Manager	Preferences	Support Action

If you have difficulty identifying the preferences of a particular manager this could be a warning sign that you need to ask about work-style preferences and ways you can support them. These simple measures take little additional effort on the part of the assistant and can immensely improve the work life of a manager.

See the Big Picture

The more you know about your manager's projects and business, the better you can anticipate needs. Take the time to learn about a variety of departmental and organizational issues. If you attempt to operate in a box—ignoring all that does not fit perfectly into your job description—you are less likely to see important trends, upcoming changes, or future needs. Step outside of that box and you begin to see many ways in which your manager is likely to need your help. Knowing organizational goals is one way to operate outside the box.

Describe the long-range, short-range and immediate goals of your department.

Long-range goals: _____

_____

_____

_____

_____

Short-range goals: _____

_____

_____

_____

_____

Immediate goals: _____

_____

_____

_____

WHAT YOUR MANAGER EXPECTS (continued)

The following list contains a variety of ways to stay informed and see the big picture of your business and organization. Select three items from the list and schedule time on your calendar to accomplish them. Can you think of other ways to stay in touch with the big picture?

❑ Read a trade journal.

❑ Read the company newsletter.

❑ Ask to attend the departmental meeting of another department with which you have many interactions—get to know how it operates.

❑ Watch a television program on business trends, the economy or your business.

❑ Schedule an appointment with your manager to review (or create) annual departmental goals.

❑ Create a master calendar showing project deadlines, appointments, presentation dates, and so on, and color-code it by type of event or by person responsible.

❑ Schedule regular meetings with your manager to update one another on project status or new business.

❑ Your ideas:

_____

_____

_____

CHAPTER

2

Assisting the Manager

ARE THEY LOST WITHOUT YOU?

As the title indicates, the administrative assistant supports and assists administrators, executives and managers. Administrative assistants often describe themselves as "the boss's right arm" You know you are serving in your fullest capacity when those you support would be lost without you. What exactly do assistants do to provide such relied-upon support?

> ► **Anticipate Needs**
>
> ► **Act as a Communication Liaison**
>
> ► **Act as a Communication Buffer**
>
> ► **Take Over Projects for Your Boss**

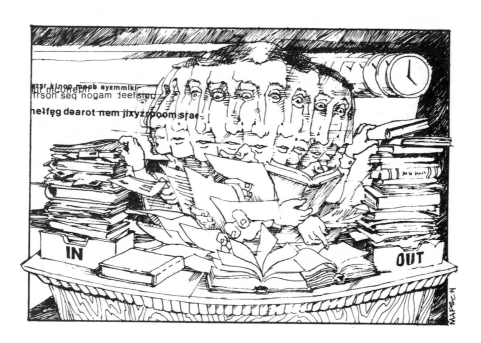

ANTICIPATE NEEDS

Recall the comedy series M*A*S*H in which Radar, the beloved company clerk, would place a document in Colonel Potter's hand the very second the Colonel asked for it. Radar was the one who routinely predicted incoming "choppers" before other ears could detect anything. The outstanding administrative assistant, like Radar, is always a step ahead of the game. For example, if the manager expresses concern that she hasn't had time to touch base with a client, the assistant assures her that the client was called two days ago. Similarly, if the boss has a meeting with a client at 3 P.M., all necessary files are in the board room before the meeting begins.

EXERCISE: Anticipation

Given what you have learned about anticipating needs (i.e., clarify expectations, know work preferences, and look for the big picture), how would you handle each of the following scenarios? What could you do prior to each event to assist your manager? Compare your responses to those suggested on page 25.

1. Your manager has a meeting with Human Resources concerning a complaint filed by a former employee.

_____

_____

_____

2. Your manager will be returning to the office today from a one-week business trip.

_____

_____

_____

3. Your manager will begin preparation of the annual budget next Monday.

_____

_____

_____

POSSIBLE RESPONSES

1. Call Human Resources and determine what documentation will be needed. Collect the full set of documentation in a labeled file. Write a summary of the file for your manager. Jot down any miscellaneous thoughts or memories you have of the case that have not been documented. Include relevant information that Human Resources didn't specifically require. Research the company policies on grievances and write a summary for your manager. Highlight policies that may be particularly problematic or useful.

2. Prioritize the mail. Check voice mail and e-mail messages. Print the messages your manager needs to know about immediately. Keep your morning schedule open. Plan a meeting with your boss, and take care of work generated during the trip. Make a list of the tasks your manager must do that day. Provide your manager with a summary of the week's events.

3. Collect necessary files, budget requests and last year's projections and outcomes. Do some preliminary figures. Create a database to ease the completion of the project. Block out several hours on your manager's calendar in which you provide absolute quiet by preventing caller or walk-in interruptions. Be available during that time, but do not interrupt.

What are some activities on your boss's plate this week? How can you help your boss prepare? What needs can you anticipate?

_____

_____

_____

_____

Clarifying expectations, knowing your manager's work preferences, and looking beyond your immediate tasks to anticipate needs will give you a "Radar-like" ability to assist your manager.

ACT AS A COMMUNICATION LIAISON

"Liaison" is French word meaning "a close bond or connection." Webster's Dictionary defines liaison as "A communication for establishing and maintaining mutual understanding." Administrative assistants are the liaisons that maintain mutual understanding and connections between managers and the staff, the public, customers and other managers.

Communication is the backbone of any organization. It is the pixie dust that keeps every operation flowing. In its absence misunderstandings and errors occur. If a manager is often away from the office the communication liaison role becomes even more critical. Unanswered questions or requests result in unhappy customers. A liaison can prevent delays. The assistant can be the hub of communication. For example, the administrative assistant in a busy marketing firm supports three representatives (who travel extensively) and the marketing manager. The three representatives rarely see each other or the manager. The assistant becomes the vital link between them.

EXERCISE: The Liaison

Identify individuals or groups that can benefit from your liaison function. Write names on the spokes of the diagram.

MAKING THE CONNECTION

Your communication skills should be outstanding; after all you are not just communicating for yourself but on behalf of your manager and your department. Many people think their communication skills are better than they actually are. A Gallop poll showed that 80% of people surveyed considered themselves to be in the top 20% of all communicators. It doesn't take a mathematical wizard to figure out that people overestimate their communication acuity. Effective communication is simply getting an idea from one person to another.

Effective Communication

Ineffective Communication

MAKING THE CONNECTION (continued)

Each communication event—whether it is a formal presentation or a casual conversation—has seven elements. When we manage these seven elements, communication is effective. When we fail to manage each one of these elements, miscommunications occur. Let's explore each of these seven elements.

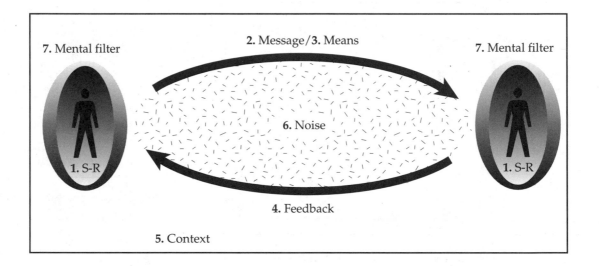

Communication Model

1. S-R: Sender-Receiver

Sender-receivers are the people involved in the communication event. Two sender-receivers are pictured in the model shown here, but there could be any number of people involved. The more people involved in a communication event, the more likely an error will occur. Many of us played the telephone game as children—one person would whisper a sentence or two into the ear of another, who would whisper to another, and so on until the last person in the group had heard the secret and repeated it aloud. Invariably the message was very different from the way it started. As communicators we need to be careful not to use the grapevine (the adult version of the telephone game—and equally unreliable). Go to the source to check the accuracy of information. Departments and department heads count on the administrative assistant to provide accurate information.

When involved in a communication event it is important to act as both a sender and a receiver. When sending a message (i.e., speaking) be aware of the nonverbal messages being sent by the listener. The yawn, the furrowed brow, the smile and nod tell us how (or if) our message is being heard. In our enthusiasm to share an idea we sometimes forget to watch for the telltale signs that a person disagrees with, or is confused, bored or upset by our message.

MAKING THE CONNECTION (continued)

2. Message

Create a clear, concise message. When delivering a message think of the clarity from the perspective of the listener(s). When giving instructions, we often rush through things because we are already familiar with the process. But this may be the first time the listener has heard about the process. The words you choose need to communicate what you mean. Avoid vague terms that could be interpreted differently by different people. For example, if a group of people is asked to write down the physical characteristics of a "short, older man" (as in, "Deliver this file to the short, older man"), the descriptions vary widely. To a 25-year-old who is 6'8", a 40-year-old man who is 6' looks shorter and older. Similarly, a 63-year-old, 5'6" individual would describe a very different person.

Avoid such words as:

maybe	probably
definitely	likely
for certain	good chance
without a doubt	doubtful

The percentage of certainty (from 0% to 100%) assigned to each of these words depends on the individual. Imagine a person who defines "probably" as 40% certainty telling a person who defines the same word as 99% certainty that they will probably get a raise this year. Someone stands to be very disappointed!

3. Means

The channel is the means by which a communicator transmits a message. Common business channels are face-to-face, telephone, e-mail, and fax. Communicators often choose the channel that is most comfortable or convenient for themselves rather than what is most appropriate and effective for the message. Use this chart to choose the most *appropriate* channel.

Message Type	E-mail	Phone	Voice Mail	In Person	Memo
Time is critical	If e-mail is checked regularly	✓	✓	If the person is easily accessible.	
Complicated message				Allows for instant feedback and questions	Allows for person to review the message for details later.
Personal message		✓		✓	
Future action is required	✓				✓
Many people need the information	An intranet e-mail system will distribute the message to everyone at once. Other systems may not.		A voice-mail system with a broadcast feature will send identical messages to many voice-mail boxes.	Staff meetings	
Personnel or legal action				✓	The Cardinal rule of all legal or personnel actions: document, document, document.
Emotional reaction may result				Although it is more difficult for the sender, giving bad news face-to-face is kinder. Good news, too, is more meaningful in person.	

MAKING THE CONNECTION (continued)

4. Feedback

Feedback ensures clarity and understanding of a message. Feedback increases the accuracy of a message and the satisfaction of the people involved. When providing feedback to others, paraphrase what they have said and allow them to correct any misunderstandings. When you want others to provide feedback to you, use these phrases:

"To make sure we're on the same page, will you run that back for me?"

"I'm not sure I've said what I meant. Please tell me your understanding."

"To make sure I didn't miss anything, will you replay those instructions?"

5. Context

The context of a communication event refers to the time and surroundings. Excellent communicators give consideration to contextual issues such as those listed below:

Contextual Considerations

CONSIDER: Have a boss that doesn't function until after the first cup of coffee?

SOLUTION: Don't set early meetings or plan to discuss important issues until after 10:00 A.M.

CONSIDER: One of the secretaries in the office gets off work at 5:00 P.M.

SOLUTION: Don't bring a pile of work to her desk at 4:55 P.M.

CONSIDER: You need to discuss a personnel matter with someone.

SOLUTION: Find a private, uninterrupted place for the discussion.

CONSIDER: You are coordinating an office retreat.

SOLUTION: Pick a fun location!

---

6. Noise

Noise refers to all the outside sounds and the mental thoughts that can disrupt or interfere with the message. We become somewhat immune to the noises of our own work environments—the phones, printers, copy machines and voices. A customer may find the noises very distracting. Arrange to have a quiet place in your office for customer or private interactions.

Mental distractions are even more difficult to deal with because leaving the room doesn't help. The internal noise goes right along with you. If you find your mind wandering, try to physically tune into the speaker. Face the person directly. Make eye contact. Nod. Focus. As your body tunes in, so will your mind. It might be helpful to take notes. Occasionally we simply need to say, "I have so much going on right now that I'm having trouble concentrating. What you have to say is important to me, and I want to give you my full attention. Could I take an hour to wrap up some things here in my office and then come see you?" (Don't forget to see the person when you said you would!)

MAKING THE CONNECTION (continued)

7. Mental Filters

Mental filters are the windows of our minds that screen all the messages we hear. These screens or filters are based on our expectations and past experiences. As with any window, if not cleaned regularly, it becomes difficult to see through it. The images become cloudy and misrepresented. If we don't keep our mental windows clean and in check with reality, we will begin to see things in a skewed manner. In a classic psychological research study, students entered a classroom for the first night of class and were handed an index card. The card was an alleged evaluation of the professor for the course. Half of the students received evaluations that said the professor was wonderful; the other half received cards that evaluated the professor poorly. The students then went through a 15-week course with the professor and at the end were asked to evaluate the professor. Guess how students evaluated the professor? Almost exactly as their individual index cards had. Although the students had been through the same 15-week course they processed it based on their mental filters.

What mental filters might you have in place. Do you have a customer, colleague or boss who has been difficult in the past? Do you have a consistently negative reaction to the person now? Consider some of the following suggestions for cleaning your filters:

- Remind yourself that a negative encounter with a person is in the past

- Give people a clean slate

- Give people the benefit of the doubt

- Recognize that people can change

- Listen to what the person is saying (not what you expect to hear)

- Give feedback (Ask, "Are you saying that . . .?")

The administrative assistant communicates effectively by managing each of the seven communication elements.

ACT AS A COMMUNICATION BUFFER

Communication may be the pixie dust that keeps an organization running, but it occasionally feels more like quicksand to the busy executive who can drown in the many requests, calls and visitors. Communication can be time consuming and labor intensive. Many administrators and executives would handle nothing but correspondence and phone calls if it weren't for an exceptional buffer. As an assistant you buffer or control communications for your boss.

Buffers have two goals:

► protect the manager's time and privacy

► provide the person contacting the manager with the desired information or solution to a problem.

The buffer role (sometimes called the gatekeeper) has a negative connotation because of instances when a manager, politician, professor or executive is impossible to reach. Overzealous gatekeepers are notorious for not letting anyone get to the president or particular managers.

It is frustrating to be denied access to information you need. Note, though, that it is the information you need and not necessarily access to a particular individual. If you get the information you need to function and perform, it won't matter if the information comes from an administrative assistant or the president. A manager who relays information through the assistant serves the customer by providing the necessary information in a timely manner with little inconvenience to all involved.

EXERCISE AHEAD

ACT AS A COMMUNICATION BUFFER
(continued)

EXERCISE: Buffer the Call

For the typical caller the administrative assistant can buffer the call for the manager by doing three things:

1. Explain who you are

2. Clearly state your offer to assist

3. Resolve the problem or answer the question

Read the following common responses to a caller.

Caller: Put Mr. Jones on, please.
Administrative assistant: One moment, please.
Problem: Transfers without attempting to resolve.

Caller: Put Mr. Jones on, please.
Administrative assistant: May I ask who's calling, please?
Problem: Fails to communicate that the caller should make the full request known.

Caller: Put Mr. Jones on, please.
Administrative assistant: What do you need?
Problem: Rude. Fails to communicate assistant status. Caller has no way of knowing that the assistant is qualified to help.

Caller: Put Mr. Jones on, please.
Administrative assistant: May I be of assistance?
Problem: The offer to assist is a request rather than a statement. Politely, but strongly, communicate that the caller should make the full request known.

Rewrite the administrative assistant's response to accomplish the three steps of buffering. Compare your response to the ones suggested on page 37.

_____

_____

_____

Possible Responses

Caller: Put Mr. Jones on, please.

Administrative assistant: Good morning. This is Brenda, Mr. Jones' assistant. How can (*not "may"*) I help?

Caller: I need to talk to Mr. Jones about the Community Arts Project.

Administrative assistant: Oh, you must be John. Mr. Jones and I were just discussing the Arts Project this morning. I have the folder right here. How may I help?

Caller: Well, I need the dates and locations for the first and second shows.

Administrative assistant: The first show is set for April 9 in the Convention Center . . .

My guess is that the next time this client calls or needs information (s)he will automatically start by asking for the administrative assistant. The buffering job becomes much easier after a few successes at providing customers with timely and accurate information.

ACT AS A COMMUNICATION BUFFER
(continued)

EXERCISE: Buffer Log

Write the opening questions or requests that the next five customers make when contacting your office by phone or in person. Write your responses and compare them to the three-step buffering process.

CALLER SAID	YOU SAID	*Did you explain your role?*	*Did you clearly offer assistance?*	*Did you move to resolution or problem solving?*

BUFFERING THE UNPLEASANT CALL

In other situations people may call your supervisor to vent or complain. These people are looking for validation of the negative emotion they are experiencing and a resolution to their complaint. The administrative assistant can usually handle both and completely satisfy the hostile or angry customer by using these steps:

> **1.** **Recognize the emotional frustration**
>
> **2.** **Apologize**
>
> **3.** **Move to solve the problem**

Read the following dialogue:

Caller: I need a purchase order and I need it now. Put the director on.

Administrative assistant: This is Ms. Director's assistant. I would like to be of assistance. What purchase order do you need?

Caller: I called two weeks ago and asked for the purchase order number to be sent to my office. I work over here at XYZ Corporation. [A major customer of your firm.] It still isn't here, and now I want to talk to someone who knows what is going on around there.

Administrative assistant: Yikes! I'm sorry that purchase order number didn't get there (*apologize*). I know this creates chaos for you (*recognize emotional frustration*). I'm so glad you've called so that I can resolve this immediately. Now, which purchase order number do you need (*move to solve*)?

Caller: I've already been through this. Now I want some answers. Put Ms. Director on.

Administrative assistant: I understand that you need this account number, which is in my database (*again attempts to move to solution*)—I'll be happy to pull it for you immediately. What was the number?

Caller: The number is 3344. I want Ms. Director to know that I'm getting sick and tired of the lousy service around here.

BUFFERING THE UNPLEASANT CALL (continued)

Administrative assistant: (*At this point the administrative assistant recognizes that the caller needs more validation and assurance or he would not still be insisting on talking to the manager.*) I will relay your concerns to Ms. Director. I know you are an incredibly valued customer, and we need to work the bugs out of our system so that you are receiving the service you need.

Caller: Darn right.

Administrative assistant: Can I be of any further assistance at this time?

Caller: (*Begrudgingly, but nevertheless . . .*) Nah, that's it. Thanks for the number.

When a customer, client or colleague of the manager has an urgent request that the assistant cannot remedy then obviously the buffering or gatekeeping function needs to be relaxed. Buffering is not message prevention; it is message screening and problem resolution. If handled gracefully and tactfully customers are appreciative of an assistant's buffering because their problems are resolved without additional transfers or delays.

TAKE OVER PROJECTS FOR YOUR BOSS

One of the most fascinating aspects of the administrative assistant role is the variety of activities. Refer to the Checklist of Responsibilities in Chapter 2 (pages 4–6). Place a "+" sign next to the items that you feel qualified for but aren't doing currently. Estimate how much additional time the selected items would take. Examine office operations and workload. Can you delegate some of your current work and expand your range of duties and assistance?

Responsibility Gray Areas

In every manager-assistant team some tasks fall clearly within the realm of the manager, some are clearly the assistant's, and some tasks or responsibilities fall within a gray area. Perhaps it is unclear how much of the manager's mail an assistant should read and answer. There may be confusion about dealing with hostile customers. When should the administrative assistant refer an angry customer to the manager?

Identify the gray areas in your assistant-manager team.

Responsibility Gray Areas:

_____

_____

_____

_____

How many of the gray areas do you feel competent or interested in taking over for your boss? Remember, nothing sounds as purely helpful to a busy executive as, "Here, I'll take care of that."

TAKING OVER WITHOUT OVER-BEARING

Suppose you have just finished reading *The Administrative Assistant* and have decided to take over attending mandatory cross-unit meetings the CEO established. Each department must be represented at this monthly meeting. Your manager has been attending and she occasionally returns with important information or presents information during the meeting. How should you go about taking over this responsibility?

DO	DO NOT
demonstrate the time your manager would save	give the impression that your manager did the task poorly
make suggestions to take over tactfully	complain about the additional time or responsibility involved
take excellent notes at the meeting	give out confidential information learned in meetings
have a back-up for yourself—never delegate a task back to your manager	delay in giving all information from the meeting to your manager
interact with other departments (you need to learn what infor- mation would be important to present)	
suggest that your manager attend the meeting with you for a trial period	
delegate something else from your Checklist of Responsibilities	

Think of a task that you would like to take over for your manager. What Do's and Do Not's would you add to this list?

Task: _____

Do's: _____

_____

Do Not's: _____

_____

Discuss the Checklist of Responsibilities (pages 4–6) and the Responsibility Gray Areas (page 41) with your manager. What projects should you take over?

Count the number of times in a day or week you are able to say, "I'll take care of it."

C H A P T E R

3

Supervising
Office Operations
and Support Staff

ARE YOU READY TO BE A SUPERVISOR?

Once there was an outstanding flight attendant. This attendant consistently received high marks on evaluations, letters of thanks from passengers, and peer awards for teamwork and creativity. So, when a new position became available, everyone immediately looked to the outstanding attendant for promotion. The manager of the attendant went to share the good news in person with this loyal employee. The manager excitedly said, "Congratulations on your promotion to pilot." The attendant was shocked and frightened. Obviously the attendant didn't have the necessary skills to fly a plane, regardless of the outstanding performance as an attendant.

This hypothetical scenario seems ludicrous. Obviously a company wouldn't promote someone into a position without the proper qualifications, right? Wrong! Day in and day out, employees (who are good at being employees) are promoted to supervisor without any supervisory qualifications. The skill differences for a support staff person and a supervisor are nearly as dramatic as the differences required for flight attendants and pilots.

An administrative assistant is sometimes given the unexpected responsibility for supervising others. Many administrative assistants report supervision to be the most challenging hat worn. How prepared are you for the supervisory function often inherent in the role of administrative assistant?

SELF-ASSESSMENT AHEAD

SUPERVISORY SKILLS SELF-ASSESSMENT

The following chart lists several skill areas. Rank your performance on each of the skill areas where a "1" means "very little skill or knowledge" and a "10" means "I'm an expert." For items ranked 5 or below describe actions you can take to enhance your knowledge and performance. Possible actions are suggested on page 50.

Supervisory Skills Self-Assessment

SKILL AREA	RANK	COURSE OF ACTION
Staffing/recruitment, interviewing, orientation		
Training of staff		
Planning and setting priorities; visualizing future of the department		
Communicating performance standards		
Monitoring and controlling group performance		
Assigning and distributing work		
Coordinating group operations		
Keeping boss and employees informed		
Motivating staff		
Delegating tasks		
Conducting meetings		

SKILL AREA	RANK	COURSE OF ACTION
Evaluating and reviewing performance; providing feedback		
Handling discipline		
Making decisions		
Managing administrative duties, including staying on top of paperwork		
Managing employee conflict		
Writing business communications		

SUGGESTED COURSES OF ACTION

- Find a seasoned mentor.

  Whom do you respect as a supervisor who knows enough about your work situation to provide valuable advice?

  _____

  What steps can you take to utilize this person's expertise and experience?

  _____

  _____

  _____

- Listen.

- Learn to ask questions.

- Review written materials.

- Observe the workplace.

- Take a seminar or business course.

- Read a book on the skill area you want to improve.

- Subscribe to a supervisory journal.

SEVEN SUPERVISORY CHALLENGES

Administrative assistants struggle with many common supervisory challenges. Select the challenges that seem most troublesome to you and read the corresponding sections.

Seven Supervisory Challenges

#1 *I don't want to sound bossy.*

#2 *People don't do things the way I ask them—I often end up doing things over.*

#3 *It's easier to do things myself than to ask someone else to do it.*

#4 *No one listens to me—I don't have the employees' cooperation.*

#5 *I don't know what to do when employees are in conflict.*

#6 *Employees go over my head.*

#7 *I have to supervise former peers.*

CHALLENGE #1: I DON'T WANT TO SOUND BOSSY

SOLUTION: *Understand your role*

If people report to you and you are responsible for distributing and evaluating work or if you are held accountable for the results of others—you *are* a supervisor regardless of your formal title. By definition, supervisors get things done through others. If you feel twinges of guilt when you say to a secretary, "Please type this up and mail it for me," you need to reevaluate your role. That is your job. Don't apologize for doing your job. New supervisors or supervisors without experience often say things like, "I hate to ask you this, but if you wouldn't mind, will you please type this up when you get a chance?" This puts employees in the uncomfortable position of trying to define the supervisory role. Although it is never necessary to be demanding or rude, it is necessary to politely make direct requests for work to be done in a particular way. Remember, supervisors are paid, not for what they do directly, but for what they get done through others.

If supervisors don't ask people to do things, the employees may feel untrusted. ("She never asks us to do anything because nobody can do it good enough to suit her!") People may feel under-utilized or under-challenged, which leads to boredom and burnout. If a supervisor hesitates to provide feedback or constructive criticism, employees will feel they are in the dark. ("I never know where I stand or how I'm doing.")

Do yourself a favor:

- Ask people to do things in a simple, direct manner.

- Don't hesitate to provide feedback.

- Recognize when it is appropriate to wear your supervisory hat.

CHALLENGE #2: PEOPLE DON'T DO THINGS THE WAY I ASK THEM

SOLUTION: *Give clear instructions*

"I gave him instructions exactly as I wanted it to be done. Then I got the finished product, and it was nothing like I expected. When I questioned him, he said, "Well, that's what you said I should do."

If this scenario is familiar to you, you are experiencing a communication breakdown. In this section we will explore ways in which supervisors can improve the way they give instructions.

Use the space below to do exactly what the following instructions say:

1. Draw a straight line.

2. Draw another straight line that intersects the first.

3. Place a large dot over the first line.

Now compare your drawing to the one on the next page.

CHALLENGE #2 (continued)

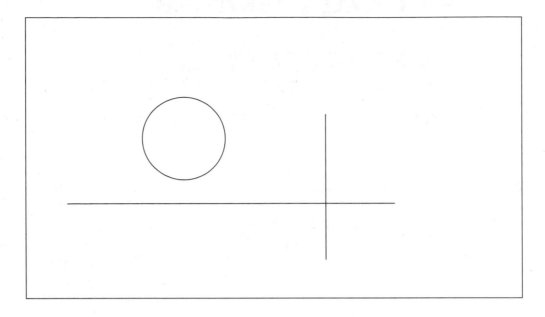

Does your drawing look like the one above? No? Why not? Didn't you follow the instructions? Well, of course you did, but there are about a million ways to interpret the instructions that were given. Could the same be true of the instructions you give at work? The following guidelines for giving effective instructions will be helpful:

- begin with an overall picture
- be specific
- number as you go
- use simple comparisons
- repeat the instructions
- show and tell the learner
- have the learner show and tell you
- check for understanding

Use these guidelines to rewrite the instructions for drawing the diagram. Compare your response to the one suggested on page 55.

_____

_____

_____

_____

Suggested Instructions

We will be drawing a simple diagram composed of two lines and a circle (*begin with an overall picture*). It does not create any particular object or picture. The two lines are going to look like a small letter "t" on its side (*use simple comparisons*). First (*number as you go*), draw a 3" horizontal line (*be specific*). Second (*number as you go*), place your finger on the right end of the horizontal line. Scoot your finger to the left 1/2" (*show and tell the learner*). This is where the vertical line (the crossbar of the "t") intersects the horizontal line. Draw a 1" vertical line with its midpoint crossing the horizontal line at the point where your finger is. Place your finger on the point where the lines intersect. Scoot your finger to the left 1/2" and above the horizontal line 1/2". Draw at this spot a circle the size of a penny (*use simple comparisons*). Watch me as I go through it (*repeat the instructions; show and tell the learner*). Now, why don't you try it (*go through each step describing what you are doing; have the learner show and tell you*). What questions do you have (*check for understanding*)?

Write out instructions for a task that you often explain (e.g., transferring a call, checking e-mail, filing, sorting mail). Give the written instructions to someone who has never done the task before and ask him or her to do the task. Watch the person. Where could your instructions have been improved?

_____

_____

_____

_____

_____

_____

_____

_____

CHALLENGE #3: IT'S EASIER TO DO THINGS MYSELF THAN TO ASK SOMEONE ELSE

SOLUTION: Delegate

Delegation is a tricky thing. If you are ultimately responsible for the work that is to be done, it is difficult to trust someone else to do it. It may be faster and more convenient to do a task yourself than to explain it to someone else. Yet over the long run, delegation will save you time and build better relationships with your staff. The following steps will help you delegate tasks more effectively:

1. Explain the need for delegating and why a particular employee was selected.

   Example: "I would like you to take over updating our departmental home page each Friday. Your World Wide Web design skills are perfect for this. Also, because you maintain the database of new customers, you have easy access to the necessary information for the update."

2. Clarify (in writing) standards, boundaries, and the deadline. Do employees complain to you (or others) that it is impossible to meet your standards? Have you ever said, "If I want something done right, I need to do it myself?" This is the perfectionist's creed. To delegate (despite perfectionist tendencies), set up prearranged acceptability standards, then get out of the way and let people perform.

   Example: "The update needs to reflect all new customers for that week. Customers should be listed in alphabetical order. Phone numbers and company association should also be listed (*standards*). If you are aware of a new customer who doesn't appear in the database, it is fine to list the customer on the Web page, but leave me a note so I will be aware of the discrepancy (*authority boundaries*). The update needs to be complete every working Friday by 4:00 P.M." (*deadline*).

3. Provide necessary assistance.

   Example: "What resources will you need to do this? What obstacles may prevent successful completion each Friday? What can I do to eliminate those obstacles? How do you plan to accomplish the update?"

4. Establish checkpoints.

Example: "I'll check in with you at 2:00 P.M. for the next three Fridays. After that I will simply expect the page to be up when I log in Monday morning unless you have notified me of a problem."

List three tasks you currently perform that could be delegated.

Task to delegate: _____

Reason I have not delegated: (*Example: components of the job need to be done by me; no time to teach someone else; lack confidence in others*)

_____

Actions to take to delegate successfully: (*Example: schedule two afternoons to teach an employee a task; ask employee to take a specific course*)

_____

Date by which task will be delegated: _____

Task to delegate: _____

Reason I have not delegated: _____

Actions to take to delegate successfully: _____

Date by which task will be delegated: _____

Task to delegate: _____

Reason I have not delegated: _____

Actions to take to delegate successfully: _____

Date by which task will be delegated: _____

CHALLENGE #4: NO ONE LISTENS TO ME

(SOLUTION: *Enlist employee cooperation*)

Build Your Credibility

Describe someone you consider credible—a person in your life whose word you never question. What has this person done or said to build your confidence? Compare your description to the verbal and nonverbal credibility builders and busters listed below.

_____

_____

_____

_____

Place a check next to the credibility builders and busters that you want to improve or investigate in your own behavior.

Credibility Builders

VERBAL: Words you say	NONVERBAL: Things you do
please	tell the truth
thank you	follow through
I'm sorry	dress the part
I was wrong	hang certificates or tasteful art in office
state facts rather than opinions or gossip	be visible and available to staff

Credibility Busters

VERBAL: Words you say	NONVERBAL: Things you do
hedges: "I'm not sure, but I think . . ."	unkept promises
tag questions: "This is excellent work, right?"	speak too rapidly, too slowly, too softly, too loudly
an awful, terrible, overuse of way way too many darling little adjectives	don't make eye contact
"It's not my fault."	show favoritism

CHALLENGE #4 (continued)

Employees who learn not to respect the supervisor position (in some part because of the supervisor's actions) can be an eternal thorn in the side. Don't invite disrespect by communicating (verbally or nonverbally) in a non-credible way.

Look through the following phrases that administrative assistants wearing the supervisor's hat have been heard to utter. Rewrite the phrases in a more credible way. Compare your responses to those suggested below.

1. I'm sure you've already thought of this, but I wanted to remind you to check the mail for new registrations today.

Problem? _____

Rewrite: _____

_____

2. Our department has the best staff.

Problem? _____

Rewrite: _____

3. This report is absolutely fantastic. I'm just thrilled and delighted with your work.

Problem? _____

Rewrite: _____

_____

Suggested Responses

1. *Problem:* Hedging

Response: Please check the mail for new registrations today.

2. *Problem:* Opinion versus statement of fact

   Response: Our department has the highest record of production this quarter. Our turnover rate is lower than any other division, and we've been recognized by the CEO as "Outstanding Performer" Award winners for three years straight.

3. *Problem:* Overuse of adjectives

   Response: This report is outstanding. Thank you.

Building your credibility is an important way to enlist employee cooperation. Here are several other suggestions:

- stand up for people (take responsibility for missed deadlines and errors)
- be as flexible as you can in meeting the needs of employees
- show a friendly interest in people
- actively involve people in decisions affecting their work
- learn abilities of individual employees

List the names of employees who report to you. Observe and record their specific strengths and interests. Cooperation is enhanced as the supervisor learns to appreciate individual employees.

Employee Name	Strengths	Interests

CHALLENGE #5: I DON'T KNOW WHAT TO DO WHEN EMPLOYEES ARE IN CONFLICT

SOLUTION: *Intervene*

Supervisors often take a hands-off approach (or a head-in-the-sand approach) when two or more employees are arguing. Rationalizing that, "This isn't my business," may allow a supervisor to avoid involvement, but a disagreement that affects performance or morale is very much a supervisor's business. When conflict escalates, a department risks turnover, lost productivity, even sabotage.

Intervention requires that a supervisor:

- call a meeting with those involved

- set ground rules (e.g., focus on behaviors, not opinions; no interrupting; find a solution everyone can live with)

- allow each person to discuss the conflict

- ask, "What needs to happen that isn't happening now?"

- brainstorm many possible solutions with employees

- get verbal or written agreement to make necessary changes

CHALLENGE #6: EMPLOYEES GO OVER MY HEAD

> **SOLUTION:** *Elicit support from the "top"*

Consider the following scenario:

> Your boss, Samantha, left you a phone message saying, "Let's order the new desk chair for Preston (your employee) that he was in here asking about last week." This is the first you've heard of a desk chair.

A frank discussion with your boss is in order. Explain to her that Preston apparently is confused about the proper chain of command. Request that from now on she politely ask Preston, "Have you run this past your supervisor yet? That's where this needs to begin."

CHALLENGE #7: SUPERVISING FORMER PEERS

> **SOLUTION:** *Clarify roles*

Consider this scenario:

> You and three other colleagues have been with the company for over three years doing similar jobs and reporting to the same boss. With your boss's retirement last year you applied for and were awarded the position. Next week you start supervising the three people with whom you have been working and eating lunch all these years. You are concerned about the relationship dynamics and feel uncomfortable about your new role.

Supervising former peers can be one of the most difficult situations a supervisor faces. Try these suggestions:

▶ Discuss the awkwardness of the situation and allow the others to make suggestions for your transition period.

▶ Pull back from socializing with them. (Remember all those lunches when you vented about the boss? They still need that opportunity.)

▶ Build new relationships with other administrative assistants/ supervisors.

The supervisory hat is critical to an administrative assistant's success. Return to this chapter often as new challenges arise in the supervisory arena of your administrative assistant position.

C H A P T E R

4

Providing Information

ARE YOU A WEALTH OF INFORMATION?

The administrative assistant will be called upon to answer just about every question imaginable—and a few beyond the realm of imagination.

What is the most bizarre question you've been asked this month?

_____

_____

An Administrative Assistant Hears It All:

Some favorite bizarre questions:

"I think there are bugs in my office—how do I get rid of them?"

"Someone's tie is stuck in the copier—what should I do?"

"Is cat scratch fever a real disease?"

The questions are worth a chuckle or two and emphasize that the administrative assistant needs to be a detective of sorts—able to find information quickly on a variety of topics.

DEVELOPING THE DETECTIVE HAT

How do outstanding administrative assistants accumulate the wealth of information that seems to be at their fingertips at any moment? These are some of their tricks of the trade:

▶ Have a background in the department in which you will be acting as an administrative assistant. If you will be working in Human Resources, have experience and a working knowledge of Human Resources information and terminology. If you will be in Purchasing, be aware of purchasing processes. Your job as an administrative assistant has a multitude of responsibilities you will need to learn and master. Don't overwhelm yourself by trying to become familiar with a new industry in addition to your job tasks.

▶ Attend project meetings even if you are not sure you will be involved with the project. You may not contribute anything to the meetings, but you will most likely learn something that can be applied elsewhere.

▶ Soak up as much information as possible from as many sources as possible. Well-informed people are insatiably curious and read constantly.

▶ Quickly translate problems into information quests. When a problem arises in your department, reframe it as a need for more information. Consider the following examples:

PROBLEM STATEMENT: ⟹	INFORMATION QUEST:
"We don't have any envelopes to fit the mailer." ⟹	"What size do we need? What do local business supply stores have? Can we resize the mailer?
"Our sales were down last month." ⟹	"By how much? What changes have we made? What changes have occurred external to our organization?"

▶ Judge validity of information and reliability of the information source. Well-informed people always prefer an authoritative opinion over gossip.

► Exhaust a variety of information resources. Do not assume after one or two attempts that the answer to a question or resolution to a problem cannot be found. Use the following resource list as a starting point for information quests:

Resource List

Telephone book

World Wide Web

Library

Reference librarians

Newspapers

Quarterly and annual reports

Databases

Company publications—newsletters/ memos/advertisements

Organizational charts

Bookstores

Local college night or correspondence courses

Chamber of Commerce materials

Company FAQs (frequently asked questions)

Journals

Training events

The answers to many questions may be as near as your telephone book. Your company directory lists various departments and gives you a good feel for what the company has to offer, where to go for help, and so on.

The World Wide Web (WWW) has an unlimited amount of information on a myriad of topics. Browsers (the software used to view the WWW) have items called search engines. You can type in a key word through one of these search engines, and it will search for documents that contain the key word.

FAQ (frequently asked question) lists can be maintained on a company-wide database, along with the answers.

Compile a list of expertise areas. Administrative assistants and support staff throughout the organization sign up as experts on topics ranging from grammar and proofreading skills to a particular computer application or "knowing how to deal with cranky clients." One phone call to the listed expert and you're all set.

DEVELOPING THE DETECTIVE HAT
(continued)

Identify three sources you could use for each information request. What types of questions would you ask?

- Your department is considering the purchase of a new desktop projector. You have been asked to gather information and make a recommendation.

_____

_____

_____

_____

- Your boss is taking a business trip to New Zealand next month and would like more information on the area.

_____

_____

_____

_____

SHARING THE INFORMATION

An outstanding administrative assistant can track down the answer to nearly any question. Just as important is the assistant's skill in sharing that information. When asked a question, don't be afraid to say, "I don't know, but I'll find out for you." File information in a retrievable manner. Sticky notes and scraps of paper with random thoughts and information aren't very helpful unless you can find them when you need them.

Give your manager plenty of information for travel purposes. When planning travel for others, provide detailed itineraries. List phone numbers next to all services being used (e.g., limo or shuttle service, hotel, airline). Include travel arrangement instructions. For example, note on the itinerary that the traveler should book the return shuttle at the same time as booking the initial transport. Include a list of office phone numbers and project files.

Shift the focus of information requests from transfer to resolve. A front-line receptionist is instructed to pass along calls to the appropriate person. Granted, a certain level of knowledge is needed to know the person to whom one should transfer the call. Yet as the administrative assistant—you are the answer-er! Calls coming in should not be forwarded automatically. When a person has a question, the assistant's goal is to access the information and provide it. Problems were once deferred to someone else. As an administrative assistant the problem will be yours to resolve.

C H A P T E R

5

Special Concerns of the Administrative Assistant

PERSONAL REQUESTS

You have been with your department for several years. Over the years you and your boss have developed a great working relationship. She treats you as the truly valuable resource you are. Last month she took over as acting vice president while a search-and-screen committee selects a new vice president. Your boss is now swamped with the work of the former vice president as well as her usual managerial responsibilities. Last week, for the first time in your four years with her, she asked you to make coffee for the staff meeting. Understanding that she was swamped, you made coffee without hesitation. Yesterday she asked you to make a doctor's appointment for her with her personal physician. Because you keep her calendar you decided it was an acceptable request. Yet you are feeling edgy that a dangerous precedent might be established. Today she asked if you would mind dropping off her books at the public library while you are out for lunch.

Perhaps one of the trickiest situations an administrative assistant has to cope with is when the boss asks for personal assistance. For example, "Will you make coffee?" or "My dry cleaning needs to be picked up," or "Could you send something to my wife—it's our anniversary." For some administrative assistants the line is clear. If it isn't work related—it doesn't get done. For others the issue of personal requests isn't as clear cut. As one administrative assistant explained, "I see my job as helping my boss so that he can function in his very demanding position. If making a doctor's appointment for him frees up his time, then I am doing my job, and it is work related." So, where's the line?

PERSONAL REQUESTS (continued)

Draw a line through any requests that seem inappropriate to you. Write in any other unacceptable requests at the bottom of the list.

drop off/pick up dry cleaning

shop for family gifts

send flowers to a client

send flowers to family

clean the car

make coffee

make personal appointments with friends, doctor, hairdresser, dentist, golf partners

return loaned books or videos

water office plants

make reservations for lunch with personal acquaintances

pick up purchases

send condolence or get-well card to clients

others: _____

_____

_____

_____

_____

How do you go about saying "no" to personal requests? Try this "no" sandwich method:

1. Yes (*explain what you are willing to do or what alternatives you will offer*)

2. No (*the "no" is sandwiched between "yeses"*)

3. Explanation (*briefly explain why you have said no*)

4. Yes (*close by restating what you are willing to do*)

For example:

"I would be more than happy to go to the meeting with the architect tomorrow (*Yes*). That will free you up to shop for your daughter's birthday. I would prefer not to do that (*No*). Something that comes from you will mean much more to her (*Explanation*). But again I'll be glad to take care of the 3:00 meeting (*Yes*).

EXERCISE: Creating Boundaries

Select one of the personal requests you would feel uncomfortable doing. Imagine yourself using the "no" sandwich to tell your manager that you do not want to perform this task. Write out what you would say:

_____

_____

_____

_____

Check your words:

❏ Did you begin with a yes or "this is what I will do?"

❏ Did you continue by clearly saying no to the request?

❏ Did you give an explanation as to why you said no?

❏ Did you end by restating what you will or can do?

WORK OVERLOAD

> You are overwhelmed. You haven't taken a lunch hour in four months. You often work late, and you always take a full briefcase home on the weekends. Your spouse has started growling about your constant working, so you are trying to smuggle work home.

▶ **Take a good look at your role and responsibilities.** Have you brought entry-level tasks with you through a promotion? Are you doing work that should be delegated or outsourced? Is it humanly possibly to keep up with your workload? If not, it is time to clarify expectations with your supervisor. If job duties change, your supervisor should communicate those changes to other staff. But what if the boss is the problem?

▶ **When your manager makes demands or requests that exceed the number of work hours in a day, explain what is on your plate and ask your manager to assist in prioritizing.** For example:

Manager's request: "Donna, would you call the committee members this afternoon?"

Assistant's response: "Sure. Let me show you what I had planned and we can decide what can wait until tomorrow. You had asked me to finish the budget request before close of business, I need to draft a memo to the COO about new computer hardware, and the meeting with the architect is this afternoon at 3:00 P.M. To call the committee members, I will need to free up an hour. How about the memo to the COO—think that can wait?

Prioritizing is a part of the assistant's role. Your manager shouldn't be expected to prioritize daily routines or ordinary projects; however, if the workload is out of control this a great strategy to prioritize the work and make your manager aware of the load.

▶ **Post a daily schedule where others can see it.** The assistant with a posted schedule is never accused of slacking. People see exactly where their requests fit into the list of priorities.

For example, one assistant in charge of computer and technical support purchased five new computers for the office. When they arrived he left them packed in the boxes rather than getting them out and setting them up. The office staff was livid until the assistant explained his workload for the week (which included some responsibilities that obviously took precedence over the new computers). The assistant also explained what benefit the staff would get by waiting: "I can't take the time right now to set these up correctly or to teach you how to use them. Give me until next week and the transition for you will be much easier." The staff agreed, without objection, that the assistant's prioritizing was right on target and that it made perfectly good sense to wait on the new equipment. The priorities had to be explained first, though!

TIME-SAVING TIPS

Multiple demands on an administrative assistant make time-saving tips essential. Here are some tried and true time-savers used by administrative assistants in a variety of organizations.

1. **Make phone appointments.**

    Example: Mr. Johnson would like to set a phone appointment with Ms. Lutz. What mornings does she have open next week? All right then, Mr. Johnson will call her at 10:00 A.M. on Tuesday morning. I'll put that on his calendar right now (*implying Mrs. Lutz should do the same*).

    Benefits: Reduces need for travel; cuts down on meeting time as phone meetings are usually shorter than face-to-face meetings.

2. **Use voice mail and answering machines effectively.**

    Example: Never leave a message that says only, "Call me back." Instead try, "Hi, John. This is Brenda with XYZ company. I am looking for the date that the National conference will be this year. Please call my office at (*phone number*) and leave a message with the dates and location. Thanks for the information."

    Benefits: The customary "Call me back" message generates never-ending games of phone tag. Leaving specific messages eliminates the call-back game. Also, call people who tend to be "long winded" when you know the machine will pick up. You can save time by leaving a message.

3. **Utilize e-mail.**

    Example: E-mail allows you to send a message that is received almost immediately (although not necessarily read immediately!) E-mail sends a message from your computer through a network to someone else's computer. You can log into your e-mail account and check and respond to messages. With an appropriate modem you can access and respond to e-mail from home or other sites.

Suggestions for Effective Use of E-mail:

- Use subject line well—sometimes messages get to the wrong person or area and need to be deleted or forwarded. If the subject line is clear, people can deal with the message without reading a lengthy message.

- Include only key points and phone numbers to obtain more information. People who aren't interested in the topic need not read through a lengthy message.

- Save up several messages and send them in one note.

- Create address books so that you can send one message to a group of individuals with just a few keystrokes.

4. **Have a five-minute list.**

Benefits: Often there are little chunks of time in the day that are too short to begin a major project. Typically these spots of time get spent unproductively. Often the five spare minutes are spent wondering, "Gee, I wonder what I could do in only five minutes?" It is surprising to see how quickly five minutes here and ten minutes there add up.

Sample five-minute list:
- file (top 15 pieces from the pile)
- skim an article
- clean computer screen
- get supplies together to begin major project later
- surf the Web for new information relevant to the organization

5. **Conference by video or telephone.**

Benefits: Reduce travel time.

Suggested Reading: Effective Video Conferencing, by Lynn Diamond and Stephanie Roberts. Crisp Publications, 1996.

TIME-SAVING TIPS (continued)

6. **Share word-processing files on computer networks.**

Benefits: No need to wait for files to be given to you on computer disk; no need to re-key information someone else has input.

7. **Make information available on-line or on a recorded voice line to reduce routine requests.**

Example: Movie theaters have done it for years. If many calls coming into the office are routine information requests, consider recording the information and making it available by phone.

8. **Color-code correspondence with a checkmark in the corner.**

Benefits: Filing is quicker and can be delegated.

Example: An assistant who supports multiple managers keeps a different color file on each manager. As incoming mail is opened and sorted, she places a checkmark on each piece with a corresponding color. The mail is routed, reviewed by managers and often returned for filing. No re-reading is necessary. The assistant merely notes the color marked in the corner and files accordingly.

9. **Save steps.**

Example: Examine how far you walk to deliver messages or documents to other people—consider relocating people with whom you interact often (so that you are closer to one another). Keep mail boxes on your desk so that people come to your space to pick up messages or completed work.

Benefits: Saves time and energy.

10. **Get rid of office plants.**

Benefits: No more watering!

Suggestion: Buy silk.

11. Create macros.

Benefits: Most word-processing systems have a function that allows you to create an entire phrase or form with a few pre-selected keystrokes. Macros may seem intimidating to a nontechnical person, but they are relatively simple to create and are great time savers.

Example: When writing this book, I found myself typing out the words "administrative assistant" time and time again. I configured my word processor to recognize the keystrokes [alt] and [aa] to mean the entire phrase "administrative assistant." By using three keystrokes, a whole phrase appears in my document.

12. Use work request forms.

Benefits: Eliminate the need to see managers prior to completing routine types of work. At a glance you can see exactly what is being requested of you.

Example: Include such things as a space for a description of the work, check boxes for standard instructions and a place to indicate the due date. A reminder of the days required for requests is also useful.

WORK REQUEST FORM AHEAD

Work Request Form

Work submitted by: _____

Date submitted: _____

Date needed: _____

Type of work requested (*check all that apply*):

❑ typing (*describe any special formatting not indicated on originals*)

❑ writing/editing: (*describe basic message intent*)

❑ photocopying

    ❑ front and back

    ❑ one-sided

    ❑ collated

    ❑ stapled (top lefthand corner unless otherwise indicated)

❑ entries to database

❑ filing

Special Instructions:

_____

_____

Work completed by _____ Date _____

Reminder: Writing and typing requests should be made three days prior to date needed. Allow two days for other requests.

MAKING TIME

Which of the following time-wasters would you like to eliminate from your day? Add other time-wasters that contribute to work overload.

1. You take calls for people when they are not at their desks. The assistant you replaced walked to each person's desk and placed the telephone message on the desk.

Eliminate this by: _____

_____

(*Suggestions:* create mailboxes near your office and use them for messages; forward messages to voice mail)

2. People often sit down across from your work station and chat about personal things.

Eliminate this by: _____

_____

(*Suggestions:* do away with the chair; continue working)

3. People see your desk first when they enter the office and ask you directions to any number of places in the building.

Eliminate this by: _____

_____

(*Suggestions:* designate a receptionist and reception area to handle walk-in traffic; post signs giving directions to commonly requested places; rearrange office so that your back is to the main traffic area)

4. Your lunch break is in 10 minutes. You don't want to start a major project, so you browse the newspaper.

Eliminate this by: _____

_____

(*Suggestion:* five-minute list)

MAKING TIME (continued)

5. One of the people you support insists on repeating her instructions.

Eliminate this by: _____

_____

(*Suggestion:* interrupt when the person begins repeating herself: "I think I have it. Let me run this back to check my understanding . . .")

6. You produce materials for several people. You have difficulty locating these individuals each time you're ready to duplicate their materials, but you must discuss with them the number of copies needed, their copying preferences (e.g., one- or two-sided) and so on.

Eliminate this by: _____

_____

(Suggestion: work request forms)

7. You take calls for several people when they are not at their desks. Often the people calling leave long-winded messages (using up to 10 minutes of your time and requiring lengthy rewrites to make the message legible.)

Eliminate this by: _____

_____

(*Suggestions:* transfer caller to person's voice mail; ask, "May I have your name and number?" rather than, "May I take a message?")

8. Other time-wasters: _____

_____

_____

_____

DEALING WITH INTERRUPTIONS

Consider the following scenario:

> Three to four times an hour your manager or one of the four support staff that you supervise will stop by your desk to ask you questions. You take your role as "information resource" very seriously. Yet there seems to be no time for you to do any thinking or mentally taxing work.

Record all the interruptions you experience in the next work day. In your mind, which ones were critical and worthy of interruptions? What about in the mind of the interrupter? How could you have eliminated some of the unnecessary interruptions? Use the suggestions on page 88.

Interruption	Necessary (Yes or No)	Means of Managing
Example: Darla stopped by with photos of her vacation	No	quiet hour; closed door = no interruptions

SUGGESTIONS FOR MANAGING INTERRUPTIONS

► Communicate to the interrupter nonverbally that you are busy (e.g., continue working, look at your watch).

► Make a habit of closing your office door when you want uninterrupted time. Work with it open at other times so that the closing means something significant to others.

► Let voice mail or an answering machine pick up the phone.

► Institute a quiet hour during which others in the office handle phone calls, customers, and manager requests while you do quiet work. Rotate one person to the reception area during your quiet hour but book no appointments during that time. Arrange quiet hours for other staff members.

► Set aside time for phone calls and consultations—for example, let office staff know that you are completely available to them during certain hours.

► Work at another location. The wonders of technology allow us to forward phones to other offices and check e-mail from any place that has a phone line. Go to the library, a quiet café or a private conference room to accomplish complex tasks that require uninterrupted time.

SUPPORTING TWO OR MORE PEOPLE

At an Annual Professional Secretaries International Conference, working for more than one boss was ranked as one of the top challenges facing support staff and assistants today. In our leaner organizations the days of one assistant per manager have ceased. If you want to be the TOPS at supporting two or more people remember these guidelines:

Treat individuals individually: Know and attempt to meet individual work preferences. Review pages 16–18 for tips on clarifying their preferences.

Organize, organize, organize!

Prioritize: Communicate the priorities for your week. If the work of two mangers conflicts, ask them to determine the priority.

Save time: Use the time-saving tips suggested on pages 80–86.

CONCLUSION

Administrative Assistant—it's an exciting career with endless opportunities. The assistant must learn to wear many hats including assistant to the manger, office supervisor, and information provider. At the beginning of this book you described your vision of the ideal administrative assistant position. You have practiced the skills necessary to expand your current role into that ideal position. Apply what you have learned in this book to your work, and you can make your vision your reality. You can be a truly amazing administrative assistant!

NOTES

NOTES

NOTES

NOTES

NOTES

NOTES

Now Available From

CRISP PUBLICATIONS

Books•Videos•CD-ROMs•Computer-Based Training Products

If you enjoyed this book, we have great news for you. There are over 200 books available in the *50-Minute*™ Series. To request a free full-line catalog, contact your local distributor or Crisp Publications, Inc., 1200 Hamilton Court, Menlo Park, CA 94025. Our toll-free number is 800-442-7477. Visit our website at: www.crisplearning.com.

Subject Areas Include:

Management
Human Resources
Communication Skills
Personal Development
Marketing/Sales
Organizational Development
Customer Service/Quality
Computer Skills
Small Business and Entrepreneurship
Adult Literacy and Learning
Life Planning and Retirement

CRISP WORLDWIDE DISTRIBUTION

English language books are distributed worldwide. Major international distributors include:

ASIA/PACIFIC

Australia/New Zealand: In Learning, PO Box 1051, Springwood QLD, Brisbane, Australia 4127   Tel: 61-7-3-841-2286, Facsimile: 61-7-3-841-1580
ATTN: Messrs. Gordon

Philippines: National Book Store Inc., Quad Alpha Centrum Bldg, 125 Pioneer Street, Mandaluyong, Metro Manila, Philippines   Tel: 632-631-8051, Facsimile: 632-631-5016

Singapore, Malaysia, Brunei, Indonesia: Times Book Shops. Direct sales HQ: STP Distributors, Pasir Panjang Distrientre, Block 1 #03-01A, Pasir Panjang Rd, Singapore 118480   Tel: 65-2767626, Facsimile: 65-2767119

Japan: Phoenix Associates Co., Ltd., Mizuho Bldng, 3-F, 2-12-2, Kami Osaki, Shinagawa-Ku, Tokyo 141   Tel: 81-33-443-7231, Facsimile: 81-33-443-7640
ATTN: Mr. Peter Owans

CANADA

Reid Publishing, Ltd., Box 69559, 60 Briarwood Avenue, Port Credit, Ontario, Canada L5G 3N6 Tel: (905) 842-4428, Facsimile: (905) 842-9327
ATTN: Mr. Steve Connolly/Mr. Jerry McNabb

Trade Book Stores: Raincoast Books, 8680 Cambie Street, Vancouver, B.C., V6P 6M9 Tel: (604) 323-7100, Facsimile: (604) 323-2600   ATTN: Order Desk

EUROPEAN UNION

England: Flex Training, Ltd., 9-15 Hitchin Street, Baldock, Hertfordshire, SG7 6A, England Tel: 44-1-46-289-6000, Facsimile: 44-1-46-289-2417
ATTN: Mr. David Willetts

INDIA

Multi-Media HRD, Pvt., Ltd., National House, Tulloch Road, Appolo Bunder, Bombay, India 400-039   Tel: 91-22-204-2281, Facsimile: 91-22-283-6478
ATTN: Messrs. Aggarwal

SOUTH AMERICA

Mexico: Grupo Editorial Iberoamerica, Nebraska 199, Col. Napoles, 03810 Mexico, D.F. Tel: 525-523-0994, Facsimile: 525-543-1173   ATTN: Señor Nicholas Grepe

SOUTH AFRICA

Alternative Books, PO Box 1345, Ferndale 2160, South Africa
Tel: 27-11-792-7730, Facsimile: 27-11-792-7787   ATTN: Mr. Vernon de Haas